TARTUFFE

Comic Opera in Three Acts

Music and Libretto
by
Kirke Mechem

Based upon the play by Molière

Ed. 3927

G. SCHIRMER, *Inc.*

DISTRIBUTED BY
HAL•LEONARD™
CORPORATION
7777 W. BLUEMOUND RD. P.O. BOX 13819 MILWAUKEE, WI 53213

Important Notice

Performances of this opera must be licensed by the publisher.

All inquiries should be directed to the Publisher:

G. Schirmer Rental Department
5 Bellvale Road
Chester, NY 10918
(914) 469-2271

CHARACTERS

Tartuffe, a hypocrite .... Baritone
Orgon, a wealthy Parisian .... Bass
Elmire, Orgon's second wife .... Mezzo-soprano
Mariane, Orgon's daughter .... Soprano
Dorine, Mariane's maid .... Soprano
Damis, Orgon's son .... High baritone
Valère, Mariane's fiancé .... Tenor
Mme. Pernelle, Orgon's mother .... Mezzo-soprano
Flipote, Mme. Pernelle's maid .... Silent

The action takes place in Orgon's house, Paris, 17th-century.

Tartuffe was written with the support of a composer-librettist grant from the National Endowment for the Arts to the composer. It was first performed by the San Francisco Opera's American Opera Project, May 27, 1980.

THE STORY OF THE OPERA

ACT I: Mme. Pernelle is leaving the house of her son, Orgon. She berates the household for not living up to the standard of "that holy man" Tartuffe, whom Orgon has befriended. Elmire, Orgon's second wife, vainly attempts to make peace. Orgon's daughter, Mariane, and her brother, Damis enlist Elmire's help in holding Orgon to his promise that Mariane may wed Valère.

Upon Orgon's return home, the maid Dorine tries to tell him that his wife has been ill, but he asks only about Tartuffe. When Elmire questions Orgon about his promise to Mariane, he evades her, then tells Mariane that she must marry Tartuffe. The eavesdropping Dorine bursts into laughter, pretending that Orgon must be joking. She ridicules Tartuffe and so saucily interrupts Orgon that he storms out.

Dorine encourages Mariane to resist her father. But now Valère arrives, having heard a rumor of Mariane's betrothal. The lovers become locked in a furious quarrel. Eventually Dorine reconciles them, and they plot a scheme to outwit Orgon and get rid of Tartuffe.

ACT II: Dorine has arranged a meeting between Tartuffe and Elmire. Damis insists on hiding to observe them. Tartuffe arrives with a great show of sanctity, using it as a perverted justification of his love for Elmire. She reproaches him for his advances but promises not to tell her husband if Tartuffe will persuade Orgon to permit Mariane to wed Valère. Damis springs out of his hiding place, swearing to reveal Tartuffe's duplicity, despite Elmire's desire only to right the wrong and avoid a scandal. Orgon arrives; Damis denounces Tartuffe; but the hypocrite so cunningly chastises himself that Orgon blindly orders Damis from the house. Now sure of his position, Tartuffe manipulates Orgon into deeding his house and goods over to him.

ACT III, Scene 1: Elmire at last persuades Orgon to witness Tartuffe's treachery. Orgon is to hide under a table, coming out when Elmire signals by coughing. The wary villain enters. Elmire professes great feeling for him, but Tartuffe demands to "savor some tender favor" as proof, freely admitting his lust for her. In spite of Elmire's frantic coughing, Orgon does not emerge until Tartuffe begins to speak contemptuously of him. The game is up, but Tartuffe merely shakes the deed of gift at Orgon and goes out, threatening that "It's you, not I, who has to leave!"

Scene 2: Mme. Pernelle returns to defend Tartuffe against these latest slanders. Her opinion changes when Tartuffe returns to oust Orgon, accompanied by an obsequious court bailiff. Orgon refuses to go, and Tartuffe leaves to call the police. The "bailiff" reveals himself as Damis in disguise, and he is quickly followed by Valère disguised as a police officer and Mariane as a special envoy of the King sent to arrest Tartuffe. The "royal envoy" enumerates Tartuffe's crimes and orders him to leave the country or be jailed. Tartuffe flees, and Orgon, confessing his foolishness, presents Mariane to Valère amid general rejoicing.

TARTUFFE AND MUSICAL HUMOR

MOLIERE'S *Tartuffe* had been a favorite play of mine for years, but not until I saw the American Conservatory Theater production of it in San Francisco in the early 70's did I realize its possibilities for comic opera. The rhymed verse, the stylized, broadly comic acting bordering on choreography made *Tartuffe* almost an *opera buffa* without music. It became one of A.C.T.'s greatest successes. The director, William Ball, certainly knew that both Molière and *opera buffa* had their roots in *commedia dell'arte;* his production reminded me of this important fact.

There are really two *Tartuffes* by Molière—the three-act comedy he originally wrote, and the five-act comic morality play he was forced to make of it in order to get it past the censors. Unfortunately, we have only the latter, but evidence suggests that the first version was a straight satire of human character. The tedious disclaiming of impiety and the *deus ex machina* ending are generally acknowledged to be unwelcome additions.

But an opera is quite different from a play, and librettists are given license to make changes not permitted in the spoken theater. I removed whatever I thought Molière had added against his will, and invented an ending which conforms as closely as possible to his own without requiring the gratuitous intervention of the king. Being my own librettist, I was able to reconstruct the play along musical lines, making further changes as I composed the music.

Molière had fun with language and so did I. He invented words, he punned, and he told literary purists that the end of comedy was to please—that his success was his justification. I have taken the same attitude as composer. The score abounds in musical jokes, parody, caricature, even musical puns. If this disturbs some purist who thinks an opera should have a rigid stylistic unity in order to be quite honest, I reply as Molière did to his pious critics: "How am I to present a hypocrite on the stage without making him perform outwardly the gestures of an honest man?"

In Molière's plays, not only hypocrites but con men (Tartuffe), dupes (Orgon), and naïves (Mariane and Damis) are laughed at for mouthing words that the audience recognizes as shopworn clichés. To get the same effect in opera, these characters must occasionally sing in styles equally recognizable as *musical* clichés. In some cases the composer must walk a tightrope between making fun of the character and letting us sympathize with the character's misguided or naive sentiment. When composing Orgon's first aria I naturally wanted to mock the stereotypes of operatic religiosity in the same way that Molière ridiculed the tone of Orgon's newly-found sanctimony. But as an aria lasts considerably longer than the spoken words, I thought it necessary to give genuine musical interest, even beauty, to Orgon's conventional posturing. And I've been pleased to find that in spite of the humor and exaggeration, this aria actually moves some listeners. Perhaps this only shows how sentimental and conventional some people's taste is; I prefer to believe that it proves music can operate on several levels at the same time. Richard Strauss, for instance, intended his most famous *Rosenkavalier* waltz as pure parody, but it was, in Norman Del Mar's words, "hailed as a true example—indeed, one of the finest ever written—of the very thing of which it was originally a satire." (Incidentally, *Rosenkavalier* is full of musical borrowings, caricature, local in-jokes and what purists like to stigmatize as "anachronisms." But so is almost every comic opera, and even some more serious works, such as *Don Giovanni.*)

Parody, including the occasional outrageous quotation, is a trenchant form of satire, whether verbal or musical. The operatic *Tartuffe*'s audiences and critics have shown by their laughter and their generous reviews that they understand this very well—only one or two humorless music critics have missed the point. One wrote a review about the "bewilderingly eclectic music" without giving any hint that satire or parody were involved. But because I occasionally parody a style (as in Orgon's aria) rather than a specific piece, the reverse of this happens more often. In their eagerness to catch all the references, listeners frequently credit me with parodying or quoting composers and musical passages that I don't even know. Relax, folks, there aren't many quotations.

The fact that *Tartuffe* is a "numbers" opera—with arias, duets, trios and large ensembles—has led some to the mistaken belief that the entire work is meant to be little more than a spoof of operatic tradition, a "pseudo 18th century opera." At the other end of the spectrum are those directors who have insisted on staging my opera in later periods because, as one of them put it, "the work is so patently 20th century American."

Tartuffe is a "numbers" opera because I wanted to revive the flamboyant spirit of Molière, which considerably predates 18th century opera. We know that Molière was a great actor of farce; it is a mistake to load onto his plays the dark "social commentary" style of the 20th century. In his preface to *Tartuffe,* Molière wrote, "The most beautiful ideas in a serious philosophy are less powerful most of the time than those in a satire . . . It's a terrible blow to vice to expose it to everyone's laughter. One can easily bear re-proof; but no one can bear to be mocked . . . no one wants to be ridiculous." Yet the idea persists in some quarters that Molière's plays (and operas made from them) must be produced with a bitter, even somber tone; otherwise they are not to be taken seriously!

And even Molière has occasionally suffered from the kind of obtuseness that cannot differentiate between parody and pilfering. It has been written and often repeated that Molière is one of the few great writers who has no style, but rather the styles of all his characters. There is a grain of truth in this but it omits the important fact that his characters didn't write the plays—Molière did. And though I have followed his example in using satire and burlesque—both verbal and musical—99 percent of the music is, for better or worse, original.

I must also point out that satire may be either witty or heavy-handed. A pun may be funny or dumb. If the Beethoven quotation in Act III did not grow naturally out of both the situation and the musical material, it would not give listeners a swift perception of an incongruous relationship and they would not laugh.

It is certainly true that one can overdo this kind of humor. Particularly in music, comic effect is not enough to sustain interest very long—not, for instance, through an entire duet like that of Dorine and Mariane in Act I. Musical and dramatic movement must be maintained or the joke wears thin. But the effect need not always be purely comic. Gentle satire can produce charm, amusement, or "set up incongruities which serve in a kindly way to demolish falsehood and reveal truth" (S. Leacock).

The composer cannot, of course, be his own judge. I can say only that I have tried, like Yeats, "to rediscover an art of the theatre which shall be joyful, fantastic, extravagant, whimsical, beautiful, resonant and altogether reckless." It sounds like a good description of Molière.

—Kirke Mechem

from program notes for Lake George Opera's production of *Tartuffe*, 1982 (revised and expanded 1993).

ACT ONE

(The scene throughout the opera is the elegant salon of Orgon's *house in Paris in the seventeenth century. As the curtain rises,* Madame Pernelle *is leaving with* Flipote, *her maid. At each of the old lady's attempts to exit, the maid must wrestle with her luggage and absurd paraphernalia.* Elmire, Mariane, Damis, *and* Dorine *stand in attendance.)*

MME. PERNELLE Come along, Flipote, come along;
I'll not stay here! Not one more day!

ELMIRE But, Mother, please! Do say what's wrong.
What makes you hurry off this way?

MME. PERNELLE What's wrong? My dear daughter-in-law,
You, who are responsible
For this pandemonious household,
These flibberty-jibberty children—
You can ask what's wrong?

Good morals here
Are sorely missed;
Good manners simply
Don't exist.

They've no respect!
They contradict!
When will you learn
To be more strict?

Come along, Flipote, I must be gone.

DORINE But please, *Madame* . . .

MME. PERNELLE You! Such impertinence from the hired help!
You ought to stick to sweeping stairs
Instead of nosing into other folks' affairs.

You interrupt
My every word.
Servants should be
Seen, not heard!

Come along, Flipote, I must withdraw.

MARIANE But Grandmama . . .

MME. PERNELLE You! My *pure* little granddaughter.
So quiet, so demure.
Well, I'm not so sure;
I've seen that beau of yours,

That what's-his-name,
Your fine Valère.
They're all the same,
And you beware!

Come along, Flipote, come along, I say.

DAMIS But Grandma,won't you stay . . .

MME. PERNELLE You, Grandson!
You play the great roue, and badly, too.
If you could spell F - O - O - L,
You'd know what Granny thinks of you.

Your speech is crude,
Your manners rude.
Why can't you be
Polite like me?

(To Elmire) Madam, you must hear the truth.
A second wife who carries on so
Is not a good example for our youth.
The way you dress and entertain,
You'll make my son a debtor.
His dear departed first wife
Did much better.

DORINE *(Aside)* She'd spoil the fun of anyone.

DAMIS *(Aside)* Won't she ever quit?

MME. PERNELLE The only moral force beneath this roof
Is your father's pious friend, Tartuffe.

MAR., DAM., DOR. That hypocrite!

MME. PERNELLE That man is holy, far beyond your mean reproof;
Selfless, sacrificing; a lofty mind
Fixed only on the fair, the fine,
The worthy and sublime.

MAR., DAM., DOR. *(Variously and together)*
That bigot! That beggar! That braggart!
Selfish! Sacrilegious!
That fake! That fraud!
That phony! That fool!
Who says that every comfort is a crime!

MME. PERNELLE Suspicious minds can't comprehend
Such purity of soul.
My son's salvation is his only goal.
Tartuffe is right to castigate your sinful life.

MAR., DAM., DOR. Tartuffe's a tyrant! A sanctimonious toad!

DORINE It's not the master he looks out for;

MAR., DAM., DOR. *(Pointing to Elmire)*
It's more the master's wife. *(They laugh.)*

MME. PERNELLE Come along, Flipote, come along at once;
I'll not be laughed at like a dunce.

ELMIRE But Mother, please,
They meant no harm.

MME. PERNELLE And as for you, Madam,
I'll give just one last good advice:
That godly man was sent to you from Paradise
To save you all from sin.

MAR., DAM., DOR. O save us, Lord, from him!

MME. PERNELLE To bring him here,
My son was wise, kind,
A Christian . . .

MAR., DAM., DOR. Your son was out of his mind!
The question is:
Which one was taken in?

MME. PERNELLE My patience is gone,
My nerves are wrecked.
When will you learn
To show respect?

ELMIRE Children, please,
I must object.
Try to be
More circumspect.

MAR., DAM., DOR. She only comes
Here to inspect:
Discover faults
And find neglect.

(MADAME PERNELLE exits indignantly while ELMIRE follows in a vain attempt to soothe her.)

DORINE When beauty's gone and charm escapes,
Virtue sounds like sour grapes.

MARIANE Father's even worse.
Tartuffe's become his God . . .

DAMIS And has his hand
In Father's purse.

MARIANE Tartuffe has changed him so,
I'm quite afraid
That Father might take back
The promises he made.
He gave his word
Valère and I could marry.
He even set the date.

DORINE Here comes your father.
You'd better find your step-mother;
She'll set him straight.

(DAMIS and MARIANE hurry out. ORGON enters.)

DORINE Good morning, sir.
I hope you had a pleasant stay.

ORGON Not at all, Dorine. When I'm away
I worry about the family.
Tell me, now, how are they all?

DORINE *Madame* has had a fever
Of at least a hundred-three.

ORGON And Tartuffe? How is he?

DORINE Tartuffe? He's hale and hearty,
Well-fed and mellow, always in the pink.

ORGON Poor fellow!

DORINE *Madame* had nausea in the night.
At supper she couldn't eat a bite.

ORGON And Tartuffe? How was Tartuffe's appetite?

DORINE Two pheasants and a leg of lamb.
He cleaned his plate and licked the pan.

ORGON Poor man!

DORINE She couldn't rest 'till it was light,
The fever racked her so profoundly.

ORGON And Tartuffe—did he sleep soundly?

DORINE From ten till ten. Then after that
He felt a little faint, and took a nap.

ORGON Poor chap!

DORINE The doctor came—her pain was hell!
He bled her till the fever fell.

ORGON And Tartuffe? Did he stay well?

DORINE Oh yes, Tartuffe is feeling fine.
He replaced her blood
By drinking up your wine.
Now both are on the mend.

ORGON Poor friend!

DORINE I'll go and tell my mistress
How pleased you are
Her pain is at an end!

(She makes an elaborate curtsy, and exits.)

ORGON That man's a saint.
How well I remember
How Providence sent him to us.

ORGON (continued) Every day at church Tartuffe was there,
Kneeling just across from me in pious prayer.
The fervor of his feeling soon caught every eye;
He'd kiss the earth, and wail, and weep, and sigh.
When I rose up to go he'd run before
To give me holy water at the door.
I learned at last the man was destitute.
(His servant told me so.) But he was resolute
Refusing alms. His modesty was such
That he would always cry, "Oh no, that's much
Too much, by half." And then and there
He'd share it with the poor. Such loving care
Deserved much more. I brought him here to live,
And finally found that peace that only heaven can give.

ELMIRE *(Who has entered during the last part of ORGON's aria)*
Really, Orgon, I don't understand
What has come over you.
You used to be a man of sense.
Can't you see he's not sincere?
It's all pretense!

ORGON My dear, your impropriety
Smacks of impiety.

ELMIRE *True* devotion comes from the heart.

ORGON And only you
Can tell the two apart?
You make me doubt
If you're sufficiently devout
Yourself.

ELMIRE Be that as it may,
There's something else we must discuss.

ORGON And what is that, I pray?

ELMIRE You promised Mariane to Valère.

ORGON I did.

ELMIRE And named the wedding day.

ORGON That's true.

ELMIRE And now you've put it off?

ORGON Could be.

ELMIRE Do you have some plan in view?

ORGON We'll see.

ELMIRE You mean, you'll break your word?

ORGON I don't say that.

ELMIRE But what could stop it?

ORGON That all depends.

ELMIRE I don't see what you're driving at.

ORGON Too bad.

ELMIRE Orgon, stop! You'll drive me mad!
You made a promise—
Will you or will you not fulfill it?

ORGON I'll do exactly . . .
As Heaven wills it. *(ORGON exits.)*

(ELMIRE throws up her hands in despair and goes out at the other side. DORINE enters, then MARIANE from another door.)

MARIANE Dorine! Has Valère come yet?

DORINE Valère? Valère who?

MARIANE Don't tease me.
This waiting makes me burn.

DORINE You have a lot to learn.
Love is a game;
Don't take it to heart.

MARIANE But what about your love—your Robin?
How do you stand it, living apart?

DORINE *(Laughing)* Listen, Mariane.
(She takes up the lute.)
Here's an old song
About that kind of man,
And what to do when he's away.
It's your lesson for today.

* Fair Robin I love and hourly I die,
But not for a lip, nor a languishing eye;
He's fickle and false, and there we agree,
For I am as false and as fickle as he.

We neither believe what either can say;
And neither believing, we neither betray.
'Tis civil to swear and say things, of course;
We mean not the taking for better or worse.

When present we love; when absent agree:
I think not of Robin, nor Robin of me.
The legend of love no couple can find,
So easy to part or so easily joined.

(DORINE runs off, laughing. ORGON enters.)

[*The words of Dorine's aria are from John Dryden's *Amphitryon* (1690); "Robin" was "Iris" in the original.]

ORGON Mariane—are you alone?

(He looks around for eavesdroppers.)

MARIANE Yes, Father?

ORGON I have a little secret for you.

MARIANE You do?

(DORINE returns. Upon seeing ORGON, she arranges always to be behind him so that she can listen without being seen.)

ORGON Yes. Now listen, child.
You've always been obedient,
Modest, mild.
And I've loved you dearly.

MARIANE I'm grateful to you, Father,
And thank you most sincerely.

ORGON To be worthy of this affection,
Will you follow my wishes?

MARIANE Of course, Father.

ORGON In every way?

MARIANE It's always my ambition
To do all things exactly as you say.

ORGON Excellent, Daughter, excellent.
Tell me, now—
What do you say of Tartuffe?

MARIANE I, Father?

ORGON Yes, you.
Now answer carefully.
Think it through.

MARIANE What do I say of him?
I'll say whatever you want me to.

ORGON Well said, Daughter.
You'll say of him
Whatever I want you to.
Then say of him
That he's kind, attractive,
That he deserves the best in life.
And say of him . . .
You'd like to be his wife.

MARIANE I beg your pardon?

ORGON Well?

MARIANE What did you say?

ORGON What's the matter?

MARIANE I must have heard you wrong.
Whom were you speaking of?

ORGON Tartuffe.

MARIANE But Father, why?
To say I love
Tartuffe would be a lie.

ORGON But not if it is so!
And I've decided
That it shall be so.

MARIANE No, Father!

ORGON The blessings of Heaven
Will shine upon this house
When he is joined to us
As your loving spouse.

(DORINE, who has been listening at the door, breaks in laughing.)

ORGON What are you doing there?

DORINE *(Imitating him)* "The blessings of Heaven—"
You mean the wrath of God,
If she must wed that ugly fraud.

ORGON This is none of your affair!

DORINE Never mind, Sir,
I knew the minute you spoke
That this was just
A clever joke!

Ha ha ha ha. I might have guessed—
It's only a joke, a hoax, a jest!

ORGON *(Furiously)* You laugh? Ha ha!
Well, when you're through,
Then you will see who laughs best!

MARIANE Don't laugh, Dorine. It's really true.
Save me, O Lord, from that pious pest!

ORGON I mean what I say,
And I say what I mean!

DORINE All right, suppose we believe this whim.
What's the point, Sir?
Why should a rich man like you
Give a sweet girl like her
To a broken-down beggar like him?

ORGON You hold your tongue!
His poverty is his halo,

ORGON (continued) And far more beautiful
Than being young.
He has no use for riches here below,
And threw away the wealth he had on earth.
And that, I'm told, was very great.
For he's a gentleman by birth,
And rightful heir to a large estate.

DORINE Oh, yes! So he told me.
But should a man so holy
Show such pride?

ORGON That will do! Tartuffe aside,
I've reason enough
To change my mind about Valère.
I hear he gambles,
And his appearances at church of late
Have been extremely rare.

DORINE Oh, yes; he has to learn to go
Only when he knows
That you'll be there.

ORGON Will you be quiet?

DORINE I can't.

ORGON *(Threatening her)* You will,
Or feel the back of my hand!

DORINE *(Meekly)* I'll try it.

(ORGON glares at her until she turns aside, then addresses MARIANE.)

ORGON Now, Daughter, as I was saying,
My only wish . . .

DORINE *(Aside)* . . . is her command.

ORGON Quiet, I say!

DORINE I may.

ORGON You will!
Now, Mariane, I've given this serious thought.
You and Tartuffe . . .

DORINE *(Aside)* I may not.

ORGON Be still!

DORINE But, Sir, you're losing your temper.
That's not a very Christian thing to do.

ORGON I will not tolerate this impudent disregard!
Not one more word from you!

DORINE *(After a moment of silence under his severe gaze)*
But I'll be thinking hard!

ORGON Think all you like,
But not another squeek!
(He turns to Mariane.)
Once you get to know him . . .

DORINE It drives me wild
That I can't speak!

(She stops as soon as ORGON turns his head.)

ORGON . . . then all your doubts will pass.
You'll find Tartuffe . . .

DORINE . . . a pompous ass!

ORGON *(Angry, but determined to ignore her.)*
. . . Although he's no Adonis,
His other qualities . . .

DORINE *(Aside)* Mercy upon us!
His other qualities indeed!
Conceit, a cheat,
Deceit, effete,
And grasping greed.

ORGON *(Turns to her—his arms folded—seething inside.)*
I see how you treat
My orders—like a joke!

DORINE *(Innocently)* Why, what's wrong, Sir?
It wasn't to you that I spoke.

ORGON Oh no? Then to whom?

DORINE I was talking to myself.

ORGON *(Aside)* One more word
And she gets a good smack.

(He stands ready to strike her, and at each of the following lines to MARIANE, he glowers at her. DORINE stands bolt upright, lips pressed together.)

ORGON *(To MARIANE)* I've quite decided . . .
You and Tartuffe . . .
You'll thank me for this some day . . .
(To DORINE) Well, why don't you talk back?

DORINE I've nothing more to say.

ORGON Just one little word?

DORINE You made the rule.

ORGON One tiny, tiny word?

DORINE I'm not such a fool.

ORGON *(Turns back to* MARIANE.*)*
In short, daughter, you must forget Valère.
Tartuffe is the man whose life you'll share.

DORINE Why don't you marry him yourself?
You'd make a lovely pair!

*(*DORINE *runs off.* ORGON *swings at her but misses.)*

ORGON Impudent wench! Vixen! Ingrate!
I can't abide this insolent talk!
She's vexed me so, I can't think straight.
I'm going for a walk! *(Exits.)*

*(*MARIANE *begins to sob.* DORINE *peeks in; when she has made sure that* ORGON *has left, she comes back in.)*

DORINE Where's your spirit, girl?
You're as docile as a cow.

MARIANE But a father has such power!
I've obeyed him so long now,
I couldn't be a rebel if I tried.

DORINE So you'll stand aside
And let it happen.

MARIANE Oh, no, Dorine!

DORINE Perhaps you don't love Valère?

MARIANE You know I do!

DORINE And he loves you?

MARIANE He swears he does.

DORINE But you just heard your father swear
You'd be that ogre's bride.

MARIANE: There's only one solution:
(Tragically) Suicide!

DORINE Yes, of course! A splendid resolution!
Just like these romances
You leave around.

(Dorine picks up a small volume from the table.)

MARIANE O cruel gods! Inconstant heaven!

DORINE *(Leafing through the book)*
I think that's found on page eleven.

MARIANE No more to gaze into those eyes divine,

DORINE Chapter two, page twenty-seven.

MARIANE The bitter cup of Morpheus shall be mine.

DORINE Exactly! One hundred thirty-nine.

MARIANE Farewell, Adieu, Lebwohl, O vale of tears,

DORINE *(Reading)* All hail, sweet Stygian shore,

MARIANE	DORINE
Oblivion calls, And Fate decrees, Addio.	And Duty hears, In Chapter four.

MARIANE & DORINE *(In canon; MARIANE exaggeratedly tragic, DORINE mocking.)*

No more, pale moon,
No more our vigil keeping;
Away, too soon,
To him, who waiting, weeping,

Shall learn, too late,
The cause of this, my sighing;
And say 'tis fate
That I for love am dying.

DORINE Two hundred twenty-eight.
And they died happily ever after.

(MARIANE sobs loudly and DORINE laughs, as VALÈRE enters.)

VALÈRE Well, well,
From this side, crying,
From that one, laughter.
What's happened here?

MARIANE Valère!

VALÈRE Mariane, my dear,
I've just been told some curious news.

MARIANE Oh? What's that?

VALÈRE No doubt some kind of spoof.
I'd like your views.

MARIANE About . . . ?

VALÈRE About Monsieur Tartuffe.

MARIANE Tartuffe, you say?

VALÈRE Yes. Rumor has it
That he's to marry you.

(All three of them try to laugh.)

MARIANE Yes. . . It's true.
Father changed his mind today.

VALÈRE He changed his mind?
You're not serious?

MARIANE Yes. He insists I do it.

VALÈRE And you?
What do you intend to do?

MARIANE I don't know.

VALÈRE You don't know?
Then there's something to it?

MARIANE What do you advise?

VALÈRE Why, marry him, of course!

MARIANE Oh. So you approve this match.

VALÈRE Certainly. A splendid catch!
Madame Tartuffe!
May I congratulate
Your brilliant choice!
Red ears, raspy voice;
Such a handsome mate
Does honor to the bride.

MARIANE I'll follow your advice!
I hope you're satisfied!

VALÈRE The way you've lied to me,
It's only right for you to be
Tartuffified!

MARIANE	VALÈRE	DORINE
You said I should! Its all your fault, you know	*I* said you should? You twist things so!	Let's see how far These lovers will go.
I'm twisting things? How false can you be?	*You* made the choice. I only agree.	"Twiddle," says he, And "Twaddle," says she. *(Pointing from one to the other)*
You just want out— That's easy to see.	You've never shown Real passion for me.	
Go ahead—leave! You're perfectly free.	*I* just want out? Then so it shall be!	Twiddle-dum And tweedle-dee.
You don't love me!	You don't love me!	

VALÈRE O cruel gods! Inconstant heaven!

DORINE Merciful Lord! Not again!

(She takes up the book again.)

VALÈRE Perfidious traitor, thou shalt suffer yet;
Some kinder friend shall teach me to forget.

(Dorine offers to share the book with Mariane, who turns away indignantly.)

DORINE Right here—page ten.

VALÈRE No more, false heart,
Shall I believe thy sighing;
Another's charms
Will soon these tears be drying.

DORINE He's easily consoled.

VALÈRE Away, apart,
O source of all my sorrow;
Another's arms
Shall hold me 'ere the morrow!

(He starts to leave.)

DORINE How beautifully expressed!

VALÈRE *(Turning back)* But remember!
It's you who drove me out.

MARIANE Of course.

VALÈRE *(Turning back again)* I only follow your example!

MARIANE No doubt.

VALÈRE *(Turns half way to the door.)*
Your wish is my command!

MARIANE Oh, yes.

VALÈRE *(Almost to the door)* This is forever, you know.

MARIANE I understand.

VALÈRE *(Turns as he reaches the door.)* What's that?

MARIANE What?

VALÈRE You called me?

MARIANE I? You're dreaming.

VALÈRE Very well. I'll go.
Farewell, Mademoiselle.

MARIANE Farewell.

DORINE All right, the play is over.
Now come to me, you two.

(During the following trio, Dorine goes first to Valère, then to Mariane, pulling one then the other toward the center. Each makes a pretense of leaving whenever Dorine busies herself with the other.)

MARIANE & VALÈRE	DORINE
I won't stay here! Don't hold him (her) back!	
It's what he (she) wants! We're through!	Come here, you two!
You heard what he (she) said— He (she) wishes I were dead!	You're out of your head!
Farewell, we're through! Farewell, adieu!	Come here, I said!

(DORINE finally gets them together.)

DORINE *(To VALÈRE)* Give me your hand! Come on!
(To MARIANE) Now yours! That's it.
(Joining their hands) A perfect fit!
Now, first Valère:
(With mock gravity) I hereby swear
She loves you.
Now give her a kiss.
(He reluctantly pecks her cheek)
Now you, Mariane:
I swear this man
Adores you.
Kiss him back.
(MARIANE returns the kiss.)

VALÈRE You must admit,
You owed me that.

MARIANE I owed you!

DORINE Will you quit!
(Gets them back together.)
Let's think now
Of stopping this terrible wedding.

MARIANE But how?

DORINE First of all,
Appear to agree;
Be as sweet
As a bride-to-be.

VALÈRE Can you do it?

MARIANE You'll see.

DORINE Once he thinks
You've swallowed the hook,
Then we'll try
Every trick in the book.

VALÈRE, DORINE Can you do it?

MARIANE By hook or by crook.

DORINE Time will be your savior;
Be on your best behavior,
But delay!
Say you'll marry him Monday,

VALÈRE But start to cough on Sunday.

DOR., MAR., VAL. They'll have to put it off another day!

(Variously and together)
We'll slow him, we'll show him,
We'll twist him, resist him,
We'll fool him, we'll foil him,
Refute him, dispute him.
Delay! Delay! Delay!

Defer him, deter him,
Detain him, restrain him,
Delay him, repay him,
Decoy him, destroy him.
Delay! Delay! Delay!

DORINE Off with you now! We'll need some help.
(To Mariane) Go find your step-mother!
I'll talk to your brother.
Now, out, I say! This way, Valère!
You, Mariane! Go right out there!

(Throughout the following trio, DORINE works just as hard to separate the lovers as she did earlier to bring them together. VALÈRE and MARIANE sing with greatly exaggerated emotion and gestures, but this time tongue-in-cheek as they deliberately thwart DORINE's attempts to get them out.)

MARIANE & VALÈRE	DORINE
No more, dear heart,	Get on! Get out!
Must I depart with sighing.	Get off! Get going!
For soon thy fears	I'll push you, I'll pull you,
Will end and tears be drying	I'll poke you, provoke you,
	I'll move you, I'll prove
	That I mean what I say!
	Be on! Be gone!
	Be off on your way!

(DORINE manages to push them out at opposite doors, then exits herself. The lovers then reappear.)

VALÈRE, MARIANE *(Lyrically, without irony)* I love you.

(DORINE reappears. They all exit, laughing.)

CURTAIN

ACT TWO

DAMIS *(Entering with* DORINE*)*
No! By the gods in heaven,
That's going too far!
May lightning strike me dead
If I don't . . .

DORINE . . . Don't lose your head!
Your father only mentioned it.

DAMIS No! It's the last straw!
I'll find that fake
And break his jaw!

DORINE For heaven's sake,
Tame that temper of yours
And quiet down.

DAMIS That hypocrite! Imposter! Clown!
I hate this phony devotion,
This holy emotion
That makes a mockery of true belief.
He beats his breast all over town,
He talks the saint but acts the thief.
I'll show this sacrilege of his
For what it is:
This rolling of eyes, these moans, these groans,
These pious platitudes,
Beatitudes pronounced in pompous tones.
Humbug! Liar! Lecher! Deadbeat!
Devil! Swindler! Charlatan! Cheat!
Just let me . . .

DORINE . . . Let me have a word. Calm down, now.
I'm on my way to fetch Tartuffe.
Your step-mother knows just how
To handle him and your father, too.
So off with you! You'd only cause a row.

DAMIS I'll stay.
I'd like to hear this interview.

DORINE No. Go away!
They must be alone.

DAMIS I won't say a word, I swear.

DORINE We know your tantrums.
Go on! You'll spoil the whole affair.

DAMIS I promise you, Dorine . . .

DORINE He's coming! Hide!
You mustn't be seen!

(DAMIS runs around the room looking for a hiding place and quickly disappears into a closet. TARTUFFE then enters, sees DORINE but pretends not to, and calls offstage to his valet.)

TARTUFFE Laurence, hang up my hair-cloth shirt;
Put my scourge in its proper place,
And pray for Heaven's eternal grace.
And Laurence, if any should chance to call,
I've gone to the prison's darkest holes
To share my bread with those poor souls.

DORINE What affectation! What monstrous gall!

TARTUFFE *(Feigning surprise)* Ah, someone's there.
What is it, girl?
No, wait! I cannot look
Until you take this cloth.

(He hands her his handkerchief while averting his eyes.)

DORINE Whatever for?

TARTUFFE To cover up that naked bust!
Such sinful sights as those
Awaken lust and soil the soul.

DORINE Your flame is easily ignited.
The sight of you without any clothes
Would leave me not the least
Little bit excited.

TARTUFFE More modesty, please, in what you say,
Or I shall instantly go away.

DORINE Oh, no. I'll go. But, Sir,
Madame has asked for you to stay.
She begs you have a word with her.

TARTUFFE Ah, with the greatest delight.

DORINE *(Aside)* That hit the mark, all right.

(TARTUFFE resumes his pious pose, then preens himself in a little mirror that he takes from his pocket and hurriedly replaces when ELMIRE enters.)

TARTUFFE May Heaven bless you, Madam,
According to the prayers of its most humble supplicant,
However sinful and shoddy,
And grant health and happiness alike
To both your soul
And body.

ELMIRE Your pious wishes are most kind.
Please sit down;
There's something on my mind . . .

TARTUFFE *(Sitting)* You're quite well again?

ELMIRE *(Also sitting)* Thank you, yes.
The fever soon let go.

TARTUFFE My prayers were much too poor, I know,
And yet, I must confess:
Every supplication I have made to Heaven
Has had but this one goal:
Your swift recuperation
And return to health in both body
(Indifferently) And soul.

ELMIRE Such solicitation. I don't deserve it.
You're too devout.

TARTUFFE Oh, that I could serve you better!

ELMIRE Now, then. There is this little matter
I wanted to speak to you about.
I'm glad that we're alone.

TARTUFFE And I, Madam, am the happiest man in France.
How many times I've prayed to Heaven
For just such a chance!

ELMIRE I want to speak quite openly.
Please be completely frank.

(DAMIS, unobserved, opens the closet door half way and watches.)

TARTUFFE As for me, Madame,
Long have I longed to bare
My soul to you.
The care I give to where
You go and what you do
Comes not from any base suspicion.
Ah, no! My passionate zeal
Makes your good name my holy mission.

ELMIRE I'm sure your one concern
Is Heaven's reward.

TARTUFFE Truly said. Ah, how I yearn . . .

(He takes her hand.)

ELMIRE Ouch! You squeeze too hard.

TARTUFFE I meant no harm.
Religious ardor made me unaware . . .

(He puts his hand on her knee.)

ELMIRE Whatever can your hand be doing there?

TARTUFFE Why, feeling your gown.
The cloth is so soft and very rare.

ELMIRE *(Moving away)* Please! I'm extremely ticklish.

TARTUFFE *(Moving after her and handling the collar of her dress)* And such fine lace! I declare,
They do such miracles nowadays.

ELMIRE Your hands find rosaries everywhere.
But back to business. You know
Mariane's been promised to Valère.
And now my husband means to break his vow
And give the girl to you. Is it so?

TARTUFFE Some rumor of the sort was in the air.
But frankly, Madam,
The happiness I hanker for
Lies elsewhere.

(He tries to look down her dress.)

ELMIRE In heavenly spheres, you mean.

TARTUFFE Like other men, I'm made
Of flesh and blood and bone.
This heart that beats within
Is not made of stone.

ELMIRE But you desire nothing here below.
That's quite well known.

TARTUFFE The love of heavenly virtue
Cannot cancel earthly love.
God's perfect works must be admired
Here below, no less than there above.
Heaven's reflected glory
Shines in miracles such as you;
This face, these eyes ignite a blaze
Of hymns in their Creator's praise.
Hosanna, Alleluia
Sings my heart a hundred ways
As it beholds in you the fairest goddess
In all God's Passion Plays.

At first I feared the Devil
Was afoot in this. Such bliss, I thought,
Must be a trap, a trial.
But soon I learned to revel
In it. Enlightened, now I taught
My heart to reconcile
Emotion with devotion,
And yield my heart to love.

ELMIRE That's quite a gallant declaration.
But do you think it suits your station?
A pious man like you . . .

TARTUFFE Pious, yes, but that's an attitude
That doesn't blind a man to pulchritude.
Why this surprise?
I'm not an angel, after all,
And even angels have been known to fall.

TARTUFFE (continued) But these sweet eyes,
These lips that set my heart aflame,
All these bewitching charms
Must share the blame
For this, if this be shame.

One look at you and I was lost,
Fiercely though at first I fought.
All my fasting, all my prayers,
My fortitude—all came to nought
Against the irresistible storm
Within my heart.
O sovereign of my soul, your reign
Shall be forever if you but deign
To grant the wish of your most humble slave.

At no risk, I might add.
Our secret goes with me unto the grave.
I'm not the sort of cad
Like all these tattling young
Virtuosi of the tongue
Who stain the virtuous name
Of those they've had.

You need have no anxiety
Where passion's paired with piety.

ELMIRE Well! You make yourself quite clear.
But have you no fear
That I might tell my husband?

TARTUFFE You're far too kind
For that. If you could see
Your sweet reflection
In the glass, you'd pardon me.
Love may be blind,
But not the lover.

ELMIRE Some wives would be
Of quite a different mind.
But I shall keep this under cover
On one condition:
You must renounce Mariane,
And help obtain Orgon's permission
For her to wed Valère.

DAMIS *(Springing out from his hiding place)*
No, Madam! No!
Stop right there!
Now we've caught the scoundrel clean
The whole world must know it.
This sordid little scene
Should be sufficient proof
To show my father how he's honored
By his faithful friend, Tartuffe!
This bigot has bullied us too long!

ELMIRE Calm down, Damis. There's no need for scandal.
It's enough if he reforms—
If he helps us right the wrong.

DAMIS No! Now he's in the trap,
He won't get out of it!

ELMIRE I gave him my word.

DAMIS Counterfeit!
Hypocrite!
This time he won't get out of it!

ELMIRE If you tell Orgon what you've heard
He'll have a fit!

DAMIS We'll soon find out—
He's coming now.

(ORGON enters.)

Welcome, Father,
We have a charming surprise.

ORGON Good day, my son.
A surprise? For me?

DAMIS Yes, really delightful.

ORGON How nice.
(To ELMIRE) Good day, my dear.
(To DAMIS) A surprise? And what might that be?

DAMIS Your wife, I think, should tell.

ELMIRE A wife is wise
To close her husband's eyes
To idle gossip.

ORGON *(Seeing TARTUFFE, who remains discreetly off to one side, praying)*
Good day, my dear, dear friend.
I hope you spent a pleasant day?
I trust that you're well?
(To ELMIRE) Gossip, you say?

DAMIS It concerns your "dear, dear friend."

ORGON I fail to see . . .

DAMIS This popinjay has found a way
To pay you back for all your love.

ORGON Our Heavenly Father above
Has a thousand times repaid it
With His blessings on my head.

DAMIS This earthy devil below
Has a thousand times betrayed it
And tried to get your wife in bed.

ORGON What's that?

DAMIS I overheard it all, just now.

ORGON Elmire, is this true?

ELMIRE Some things are better left unsaid.

DAMIS Madame, don't be so mild!
Your virtuous name compels
It! Give this devil his due!

ELMIRE A virtuous woman defends
Herself.
On that alone depends
Her honor—
Not on what she tells.

(ELMIRE retires to the opposite side of the room from TARTUFFE.)

ORGON *(To TARTUFFE)* Is this to be believed?

TARTUFFE Yes, Brother, I am wicked, guilty,
Unworthy . . .

DAMIS Don't be deceived
By this fake humility,
This sham.

TARTUFFE Ah, wretched sinner that I am,
Miserable villain! Heap on me
Your scorn; abuse me; call
Me scoundrel, demon, monster—
I deserve them all.
Whatever crime they charge me with—
I'll not deny it. Deride me,
Drive me from your sight;

DAMIS Don't fall for this ridiculous pose!
Don't let him lead you by the nose!

TARTUFFE Spurn me, Brother,
I've earned all that and more.
No matter what they say, they're right.
I'm rotten to the core!

(ORGON is much moved. He turns suddenly to DAMIS.)

ORGON *(To DAMIS)* Traitor!

DAMIS *(Incredulously)* I?

ORGON How dare you try to stigmatize
This saintly man's pure name?

DAMIS What? I saw it all with my own eyes.
Don't tell me I'm to blame!

TARTUFFE Brother, believe your son, not my poor lies.
Let me depart in shame!

ELMIRE *(Aside)* But why should lust cause such surprise?
We women know that men are all the same.

ORGON *(To Damis)* Silence! One more word from you
And I'll break every bone . . .

TARTUFFE Brother, in God's name, please!
It pierces me to hear this angry tone.
I'd rather suffer any pain
Than cause the boy a single scratch.
I beg you on my knees,
Pardon him, and punish me alone.

(Orgon throws himself on his knees with Tartuffe.)

ORGON Such goodness!
I beg you, Brother, rise.

DAMIS I can't believe my eyes.

ORGON Silence! I know your motives.
You hate him! Children, servants, wife—
You're all against him, and try to drive
This holy man away.
Well, mark what I say:
The more you strive
To drive him out,
The more I'll bend my will
To keep him in!
And I'll begin by making him
My son-in-law this very day!

(Mariane, Valère and Dorine, who have been listening at the door, burst into the room.)

MARIANE Father, please!

VALÈRE I beg you, sir!

DAMIS He's mad, I tell you.

ELMIRE Orgon, think of her.

DORINE He'd gladly sell his daughter
For Heaven's reward.

ORGON Enough, I say!
I am lord of my own house,
And I shall be obeyed!
(Softer, to Mariane)
You're just a child, my dear,
And cannot know
What joy this marriage will bring.

MARIANE Father, I beg you, hear me.
If tears have any power to move,
If Heaven, which knows my grief,
Can help me sway you from this course,
Then hear me, Father; hear the child
Of happier days. Don't take away
The life you gave. Don't force
The heart where it can only disobey.
If tears have any power to move,
If Heaven, which knows my pain,
Can touch you, Father, set me free.
Give your love, that love may love remain.

ORGON *(To himself)* Now, now, we must beware
Of human weakness.

MARIANE At least, Father, I beg you,
If I am not to have Valère,
Don't make me take a man I hate.

ORGON The more you mortify your mortal senses,
The more you'll merit Heaven's recompenses.

DAMIS This is outrageous!
You'd force that lecherous
Leech upon your own daughter?

ORGON Yes! This very night
She'll wed Tartuffe to spite
You all! And you, for your treacherous
Acts against this saintly man,
Bend your knee
And beg that he
Forgive you if he can!

DAMIS Ask that pompous pig
To pardon me? Never!

ORGON Then leave this house
Forever!

DAMIS	ORGON	TARTUFFE
All right, I'll go!	A stick, a cudgel!	
But he's a liar, a lecher!	Don't hold me back!	No, Brother, no.
The man's a monster,		
a maniac!	You dare attack	Forgive him, Brother.
Phony! Fraud!	This man of God?	
Larcenous lout!	Leave this instant!	
	Out! Out! Out!	

ORGON I disinherit you!

(Damis goes to the door, but does not leave.)

ELMIRE *(Going to Orgon)* Hold on a moment, dear.
Is this a Christian thing to do,
To cast aside your only son?
Should not a reverent man like you

ELMIRE (continued) Forgive him, even had he done
What you accuse him of?

(To Tartuffe) And I appeal to you, Sir, too,
To show a little Christian love.
Should not you, a pious man, make peace
Between your benefactor and his son?
And if he sends away Damis,
Aren't you in fact the one
Who ought to plead his case?

(Softly, to Tartuffe alone) I thought this little scene today
Might help convince you he should stay,
And might help you, with Christian grace,
(So all can hear)
Renounce my husband's wedding plan:
Restore Valère to Mariane.

(They look at Tartuffe hopefully, expectantly. He turns away with a pained, tragic gesture.)

TARTUFFE Alas, Madam, I wish with all my heart
The boy could stay. For my part,
I've pardoned him. You can't know how it
Hurts that I can't serve him better.
But Heaven's interest won't allow it.
Scandalous tongues would wag. They'd say
Such tolerance must be proof of guilt.
They'd say I try to buy his silence.
No, Madam . . . *(sobbing)* If he should stay,
God wills that I must go away.

ORGON Ah, Brother, no!
Compose yourself.
(To Damis) Villain!
I told you to go!

TARTUFFE You see what trouble I bring;
I must leave you.

ORGON No, never!

TARTUFFE They all hate me here.
The boy has sown the seed of doubt.

ORGON No! I honor you.
I cast him out!

TARTUFFE Too late, my friend. You, too,
Will soon despise me.

ORGON Never!

TARTUFFE Ah, Brother, a husband's wife
Can work upon his mind
In subtle ways.

ORGON Upon my life,
You'll stay!

TARTUFFE Well, then, if it must be;
For friendship's sake
I'll sacrifice myself.
But, Brother, it would be a grave mistake
To give the merest cause for gossip.
I'll take such pains to act discreetly
That I'll avoid your wife completely.

ORGON No! You'll see her day and night!
It pleases me to spite them,
And I shall double their despair:
Before this day is through
I'll deed my whole estate to you.
My son-in-law-to-be, I hereby swear
You'll also be my legal heir!

ELMIRE *(To Tartuffe)* Surely, Sir, you'll not accept?

TARTUFFE Madam, I must make
One thing perfectly clear:
Whatever I do, I do
For Heaven's glory, not my own.

DAMIS Leave off your high-flown
Oratory. Will you or won't you
Take what's ours?

TARTUFFE If I accept this martyrdom,
This wealth, these lands,
It's only to prevent such power
From falling into evil hands.
Weaker wills might well abuse
The wealth that I for God will use.

ORGON You'll accept it then, my son?

TARTUFFE Heaven's will be done.

ORGON Poor man!

(Orgon goes to the desk and takes out many long sheets of paper.)

ORGON
Parchment. . . pen. . . ink.
One marriage contract. Hah!
Everything I need to draw
the deed. *(Writing)* I,
Orgon Pernelle, do hereby
exercise my legal right,
In accordance with all duly
sanctioned precepts,
By all lawful canons, codes,
and regulations,
All statutory laws and bylaws.
I claim my legal right!
Now let them burst with spite!

TARTUFFE *(Kneeling in prayer)*
O Father, lead
Them from eternal night
Unto the righteous path
Of Heavenly light.
Forgive this breed
Of sinners even as I
Forgive their wicked creed.
Make them contrite,
Their souls pure white;
And may this contract,
O Lord, be air-tight.

DAMIS
What grasping greed!

ORGON (continued)
By every duly constituted
royal enactment whatsoever,
Be they constituted, canonized
or sanctioned
Under royal decree or lawful
civil statute,
I declare by every legal order
Whatsoever, howsoever.
Therefore be it decreed,
This deed shall supersede
All deeds precedent,
Ante-, retro-, inter-cedent,
Whatsoever, howsoever, wheresoever,

Be it this or any other
jurisdiction,
Any province or department
or dominion,
I do now hereby disavow,
Dispossess,
Disinherit
All of you,
All kindred whosoever!
I do swear this deed is
duly executed.
I declare all statements
therein to be truthful.
In witness whereof I here-
unto sign this deed.
I hereby claim my legal
right!
Now let this household
burst with spite!

TARTUFFE (continued)
That pompous parasite!
He won't get away with this
Without a fight.
Go on and write!
We'll fight you day and night.
We'll intercede,
We'll break the deed!
We'll plead, impede,
We'll cite, indict
You day and night.
You won't succeed
Without a fight!

MARIANE, VALÈRE, ELMIRE
Father, / Please, sir, / Orgon, — I beg you, heed
Your daughter's pleading.
Hear us, we implore you,
Open your heart. Unite
The pair that kneels before you.
Ah, world, weep for us (them)—
Weep for love that cannot be.
Neither faith nor love's delight
Can live by harsh decree.

DORINE
Ha ha ha ha. I've never seen quite
Such a marvelous sight.
They sigh and they pray,
They cry and they plead,
And I try not to laugh.
Oh how it makes the heart bleed!

(ORGON) I hereby grant, give, bestow and donate all goods, estate and property, from this day forth, for all time, from now until the end of the world, to my dear friend and only heir, Monsieur Tartuffe!

THE FAMILY No!

ORGON Yes! Yes! Yes!Yes! Yes!
Tartuffe is now my only son!

TARTUFFE *(Still kneeling in prayer)*
Forgive them, Father,
They know not what they've done.

(ORGON furiously drives the family out of the room.)

CURTAIN

ACT THREE
Scene 1

ELMIRE *(Alone)* How strange men are.
And stranger still
That women need them so.
We cannot know them,
Nor be much more to them
Than strangers, too.
But still . . .

Who can bear to live alone?
Not I.
Any pain can be borne
But the pain of lonely nights,
And any foolishness forgotten;
But not emptiness.
Yet why?
Why is an empty heart so heavy, aching,
Bearing down upon the soul,
Pressing out the blood,
The breath of life until the spirit
Suffocates?
How strange it is that pain
Should be preferred.

So be it. It can't be changed.
What a myth is marital bliss!
Such a lie!
What can a woman do about this?
We try;
We do what we can:
Give in, give out,
Give that, give this,
And give up all hope
Of marital bliss.
Give that, give this,
Give way, give ground;
Give up all hope
Of marital bliss—
It will never be found
With a man.

(ORGON enters.)

ELMIRE Orgon, I'm amazed!
This man has bewitched you.
You're not even fazed
By what he tried to do.

ORGON You're partial to that rascal son of mine
And did not dare to disavow his lie.
Besides, you were much too calm.
A woman so abused would scream and cry.

ELMIRE Oh, does every extra-marital sigh
Require martial law? Must war
Be waged? And must we scratch out the eyes
Of every amorous bore?
Laughter is the best reply.
I can't abide these virtuous vixens
Ready to spring with teeth and claws
At any man for any cause.
A cool rebuff
Is quite enough.
Laughter is the best reply
To every extra-marital sigh.

ORGON I know what's right.
Nothing will shake me.

ELMIRE What will it take
To make you see the light?
Suppose you saw the thing
With your own eyes?

ORGON Saw it?

ELMIRE Yes.

ORGON Impossible!

ELMIRE No. If I devise
A way to make you see it
Clear as day . . .

ORGON Poppycock!

ELMIRE Suppose we hide you here
Where you can see
His lustful litany all too clear.
What would you say to that?

ORGON Nothing. It couldn't be.

ELMIRE You've been deceived
And I've been disbelieved
Too long.
It's finally time
You saw and heard
How wrong you've been.

ORGON All right!
I'll take you at your word.
Let your tricks begin!
You'll soon feel quite absurd.

ELMIRE Dorine! Send in
Monsieur Tartuffe.

ELMIRE	ORGON	DORINE
(Pushing Orgon) Down here! Beneath this table. Quickly now! You must be hidden, Do as you're bidden! Get down! Do as I say!	 What? Pray tell me how. Why under there? I'm much too tall It's much too small. This is ridiculous!	 You have no time to spare! He's on his way! He's cunning, He's crafty, He's hard to catch.
Oh, no. He'll catch himself On his conceit. I've never met A lover yet Who's hard to cheat. Get down! Now stay! Not a sound! I said, "Get down!"	 What's that you say?	 I'll go this way And try to slow him down. *(Runs out.)*

ELMIRE Now don't be shocked
At anything I do or ask.
It's all to make this hypocrite
Take off his mask.
It's not at all my fashion
To invite illicit passion,
But you're the one
Who caused this course, you know.
And you're the one
To say how far you'll let it go.

But spare me, please;
The minute you hear me cough . . .
That means he's getting out of hand
And you must cut him off.
Here he comes! Do you understand?
It's up to you to stop him.

(ORGON disappears behind the tablecloth which hangs over the edge of the table under which he is hiding. DORINE ushers in TARTUFFE, then exits.)

TARTUFFE *(Coldly)* I'm told you wish to see me here.

ELMIRE Yes. A secret for your ear
Alone. But first go shut the door
And look about for spies.

(TARTUFFE goes to shut the door, looking about suspiciously, then returns and looks expectantly at ELMIRE.)

ELMIRE We can't afford to be surprised
Again. I've never suffered more
For any man! How I feared for you!
Damis upset me so, I hardly knew
What I was doing. As for the rest,
Everything has happened for the best:
It's now my *duty* to see you day and night!

ELMIRE (continued)
My husband worships your very name;
There we agree—I feel quite the same
And can't imagine any more delight
Than being locked up like this:
No risk, no fear, no blame.

TARTUFFE
Madam, you'll pardon me for seeming confused.
This morning those were not the words you used.

ELMIRE
Ah, how little you know a woman's heart!
How poorly you read the feeble art
With which we try to hide our true
Emotions. Within, the flame
Burns hot, but modesty and shame
Prevent the glow from showing through
Too quickly. And while I'm being so bold,
Consider: Why else would I have told
Damis to hold his tongue? Could I
Have heard your love so long declaimed
Had I not also been inflamed?
And when I begged you to deny
My husband's foolish wedding plan,
Could you not see that Mariane
Had made me jealous? Ah, how like a man
To misconstrue the whole affair!
Love is selfish. Love cannot share.

TARTUFFE
Ah, Madam, such music as this
From lips so sweet
Surpasses all wordly bliss.
And yet . . . you won't take it amiss
If I'm so indiscreet
To suspect there's a trick in all this?
To break off the match—
Could that be the catch?
My heart needs a pledge more concrete.

(He tries to take her in his arms but she moves away, coughing.)

Until I savor
Some tender favor . . .
Tartuffe
Requires proof.

ELMIRE
But why so fast?
Would you exhaust my store
Of tenderness so soon?
(She coughs.)
I've lost my modesty;
Must you have more?

TARTUFFE
The less we merit,
The less we dare to trust
In idle words. Before
Believing such a pretty speech,
I must be sure
You practice what you preach.

ELMIRE *(Cough)* Your passion overwhelms me.

ELMIRE (continued) *(Cough)* How can you doubt my love?
Now that I've confessed it,
A gentleman wouldn't test it. *(Cough)*

TARTUFFE I'll believe it
When I receive it.

ELMIRE *(Cough)* This is a tyrant's love!
But don't you fear
That wrath of God
You're always talking of?

TARTUFFE If Heaven is all
That blocks my way,
Forget it. That need not stay
Your heart an instant.

(During this speech, he has taken off the large cross he wears.)

ELMIRE *(Cough)* But the Bible?
Doesn't the Bible say . . .

TARTUFFE A trifle, Madam.
Drop this bourgeois naiveté
And learn the modern way
Of overcoming scruples.

ELMIRE *(Cough)* Must all your pupils
Pay this price?
Aren't you afraid of Judgment Day?

TARTUFFE There may be joys that Heaven denies,
But there's a science of compromise
That's my metier.

ELMIRE I see.
And I'm to be your protegée?

(She coughs ever louder.)

TARTUFFE Your cough is very bad.

ELMIRE Yes, it's terrible today.

TARTUFFE Would you like some licorice?

ELMIRE It will take more than licorice
To make this go away.

TARTUFFE It's very trying.

ELMIRE Yes, more than I can say.

TARTUFFE In any case, Madam,
With me the risk is very small.
Since only scandal makes a sin,
Secret sin's no sin at all.

(He moves toward her again. She avoids him, until finally she stops near the table under which ORGON is hiding. TARTUFFE advances toward her slowly. ELMIRE, coughing, directs her lines more to ORGON than to TARTUFFE, who becomes ever more bold.)

ELMIRE Well, it seems I must give in.
I simply cannot put you off.
It's quite against my will.
I do hope this dreadful cough
Is not disturbing anyone.
Some people won't believe a thing
Until they see it done.
I know it's wrong to do it . . .
So much the worse for him
Who drove me to it!

TARTUFFE If there be any blame,
I'll take it all.

ELMIRE Open the door. See if my husband
Is there in the hall.

TARTUFFE That fool? Don't give it a thought!
I've led him by the nose so long
That even if he caught
Us in the act, he'd see no wrong.

ELMIRE Still . . . go look around.

(TARTUFFE goes out, as ORGON emerges from under the table, nearly paralyzed with astonishment and rage.)

ORGON The man's a perfect monster!

ELMIRE What? Coming out so soon?

ORGON He's a devil in disguise!

ELMIRE Now don't be premature!

ORGON I can't believe my eyes.

ELMIRE Appearances deceive;
Better wait until you're sure!

(She hears TARTUFFE returning and quickly places ORGON behind her. TARTUFFE enters and advances slowly toward ELMIRE.)

TARTUFFE Heaven is with us!
I've searched the place
From end to end.
At last, my ravished soul . . .
(He opens his arms wide.)
At last, I've reached my goal . . .

ORGON *(Stepping out)*
Not so fast, my holy friend!

ORGON (continued)

So! You'd seduce my wife,
Deflower my daughter . . .
It sounds more like a layman's life
Than that of a saint!

<table>
<tr><th>TARTUFFE</th><th>ORGON</th><th>ELMIRE</th></tr>
<tr><td>(Assuming his pious attitude)
Surely, Brother,
You can't believe
That I . . .

But my intention . . .

I only tried . . .</td><td>Too late!
I saw and heard
It all—
Every wicked word!
I heard you call
Me fool!
You've lied to me,
Derided me,
Deceived me.
Well, finally, Sir,
I'm satisfied!
No more! Get out
of here at once!</td><td>That's not a part
I like to play;
Too many men
Get carried away.</td></tr>
</table>

ORGON *(Spoken)* I've long suspected you!

TARTUFFE *(Abruptly dropping his pose)*
Oh, no, my foolish dunce!
These clever stunts
To pick a quarrel
And get me out of sight
Are vain against my moral
And lawful rights!

(He takes the deed from his pocket and waves it in front of ORGON's face.)

This house,
And all your land,
Whatsoever, wheresoever,
Legally belong to me!
It's time to stop this make-believe;
It's you, not I, who has to leave!
You'll see!

(TARTUFFE strides out angrily. He pauses at the door to shake the deed threateningly at ORGON again, then rushes out. ORGON collapses in despair.)

CURTAIN

Scene 2

(Later the same day. ORGON, ELMIRE and DORINE are receiving MADAME PERNELLE, who is just entering.)

MME. PERNELLE What's this I hear?
Gossip and rumor—
What's it about?
Our family honor
Must not be in doubt!

DORINE Our godly roomer,
So good, so devout,
Has gone to the devil;
He's kicking us out.

MME. PERNELLE What's that? What's that?
What are you saying?
You cannot mean Tartuffe?

DORINE Everything is his now
That's under this roof.

MME. PERNELLE You're talking nonsense.
How can that be?

ELMIRE *(To ORGON)* If I had only known
You gave him the deed!

MME. PERNELLE (To ORGON) You know that holy man;
Explain this to me.

ORGON Mother, I'm afraid it's all too true.
I treated him like a brother,
Gave him house and home and daughter.
But the villain had to have Elmire, too.

DORINE Poor man!

MME. PERNELLE That simply is not possible!
Someone has made a terrible mistake.

ORGON Mother, for Heaven's sake,
I witnessed the whole rendezvous!

MME. PERNELLE I thought I taught you
Everything is
Not what it seems,
And virtue is the victim
Of envious schemes.

ORGON *(With increasing anger)*
Mother, that may be perfectly true,

But what can it possibly have to do
With what we're talking about?

MME. PERNELLE There's no need to shout.
I know that martyrs
Always were despised.

ORGON Mother, I saw it with my own eyes!
Saw it! S - A - W, saw!
Do you grasp what I mean?
I hid right there
And caught the rascal clean!

MME. PERNELLE If only you had waited longer . . .

(They are interrupted by a loud knocking at the door.)

ORGON What's that?

(The knocking continues.)

DORINE *(As she goes to open the door)*
It sounds like Fate
Knocking at the door.

(DORINE lets in DAMIS, disguised as an old bailiff of the court, and with him, TARTUFFE. Throughout the following scene, TARTUFFE remains aloofly in the background, content to let the "bailiff" do his dirty work. He strolls about, greedily appraising his newly acquired property.)

DAMIS *(To DORINE, in the croaking voice and accent of an old rustic)* Good evening, child.
Is the master home, I pray?

DORINE He's very busy now.
(Trying to keep them out)
Come back some other day.

DAMIS Ah, yes, but I'll allow
He'll welcome a call
From an old family friend.

DORINE Your name?

DAMIS Monsieur Loyal.
I served his father years ago.

(DORINE goes to ORGON, who, with ELMIRE and MME. PERNELLE, has been at one side, out of sight of the entrance.)

DORINE Tartuffe is here
With some old crow.

DAMIS *(Calling to them)* I've come to do
A favor, you know.

ORGON *(To ELMIRE)* Someone, perhaps,
To reconcile us.

ELMIRE You mean, exile us.

Go slow.

DAMIS *(Coming in)* Good evening, Sir.
Good evening, Ma'am.
May Heaven bless your friends
And blast your foes.

DORINE *(Aside)* That smells
Like last week's rose.

ORGON *(To ELMIRE)*
I think he's come to make amends.

DAMIS Your family's long been dear to me.

ORGON Excuse me, Sir, I'm filled with shame—
I can't recall your face or name . . .

DAMIS Loyal's the name; thank you kindly, Sir.
I'm Bailiff to the court.
And now, if you'll permit,
I have to serve you with this writ.

ORGON What?!

DAMIS Now, now, Sir. It's nothing
To get upset about.
Just a little summons
To move your family out.

ORGON Then it's so!

DAMIS Sir, as you well know,
This house and land,
Free and clear,
Now all belong to this good gentleman here.
You signed the deed
This very day.

(TARTUFFE pulls out the deed and smugly waves it at the family. The "BAILIFF" makes a motion to take it into his own hands, but TARTUFFE warily draws it back and puts it away.)

DAMIS It's quite correct
In every way.
So please, Sir, as I hold your family dear,
Be a good citizen; don't interfere.
Kindly remove yourself, your goods and kin,
And let the legal owner move right in.

ORGON	DORINE
The legal owner? Nonsense!	
Get this rascal out	And so devout he was
Before I smack his	An hour ago!
Supercilious snout!	

MME. PERNELLE	ELMIRE
I'm simply stunned	

That so holy a gentleman
Ever could treat us so!

What simpletons all of us were
To allow him to cheat us so!

ORGON Remove that villain, Sir,
Or I warn you—
Anything that might occur
Is on your head.

DAMIS Dear me, Monsieur,
I'll have to make a note
Of what you said.
Monsieur Tartuffe,
You'd better come with me.
Such defiance
Of official court decree
Must promptly cease!
Heaven knows I've tried to help you;
We'll soon be back with the police!

(DAMIS and TARTUFFE go out, slamming the door behind them.)

ORGON Well, Mother,
Was I right or not?

MME. PERNELLE I'm simply flabbergasted!
Whoever would have thought
Our good Tartuffe . . .

DORINE But Madam, don't you see?
This act is merely proof
He longs for your salvation.
As money is the root of all evil,
He's delivered all of you from temptation.

(DAMIS returns, still disguised, but without TARTUFFE.)

DAMIS *(Unctuously, as before)* Good evening, friends.

ORGON What's this?

ELM., DOR., M. PER. Leave us in peace!

DAMIS *(As he slowly removes his disguise)*
What? Not one of you can recognize
Old family friends through this disguise?
Your own . . . Damis?

ALL OTHERS Good Lord . . . Damis!

DAMIS Now listen closely! I've sent Tartuffe on alone. He'll find an officer down the road and bring him here. But don't worry—the officer is another old family friend!

ORGON What kind of crazy plot . . .

DAMIS We've got to get that deed!

ELMIRE But you'll be caught!

DORINE Look here, Damis:
Where is the real bailiff?

ORGON And the real police?

DAMIS We've sent them off
On a wild goose chase.

ORGON But they'll be back!

DAMIS That's right; it's a race.
We haven't a moment to lose.

ORGON But how can this succeed?

DORINE, ELMIRE Tartuffe can go to the law.

DAMIS Not if he thinks that we are the law.

DORINE And not if he has no deed!

DAMIS Bravo, Dorine! All of you, now, play dumb!

(He disguises himself again.)

ELMIRE Here comes Tartuffe!

DAMIS Careful now; play your parts!
There's better yet to come.

(Enter Tartuffe with Valère, disguised as a police officer.)

TARTUFFE *(Pointing at Orgon)* That's the man, Officer.

VALÈRE Monsieur Orgon Pernelle—
In the name of our noble king,
You are under arrest!

TARTUFFE If he tries to protest,
Take him to his cell!

(While Tartuffe is laughing wickedly, Valère quickly reveals his identity to the others; they fall in with the game, reacting with exaggerated despair.)

ORGON Traitor! Villain! Judas!

MME. PERNELLE And you his guest!

DAMIS *(To Orgon)* Sir, I think it's best
You come along.

TARTUFFE His abuse is in vain. I'll suffer any wrong
For Heaven's holy light.

DORINE Isn't it odd? He speaks of God

As though he owned the copyright.

ORGON Ungrateful fraud!
Does all my kindness, then,
Not count for anything?

TARTUFFE You may have given some help, that's true.
But now my duty is toward my king,
To law and order, not to you.
My country's honor won't permit
The slightest compromise with it.

DORINE How nice to be a hypocrite!
What you say and what you do
May be exactly opposite.

TARTUFFE Enough of this hullabaloo;
(To VALÈRE) Kindly serve the writ!

(Fanfare. Enter MARIANE disguised as an envoy from the king. She is elaborately dressed as a nobleman, and may be accompanied by STANDARD BEARERS, also regally dressed.)

MARIANE *(Grandly, with exaggerated French accent)*
Mesdames et Messieures:
Greetings from your gracious king!
As his special envoy,
These are the instructions I bring
For the prosecution
Of his righteous retribution!

ALL OTHERS *(Led by DAMIS and VALÈRE)*
All hail our noble king!
To thy majestic name we sing!

MARIANE Our sovereign is angry, with very just cause.
A scoundrel here has dared to defy his laws.

TARTUFFE Your grace has come with perfect speed.
There's the scoundrel there.
Kindly read this lawful deed
And put an end to this affair.

(TARTUFFE draws out the deed and hands it to MARIANE, who pretends to study the document with much mumbling of its legal terminology.)

MARIANE This seems to be in order.
It's all the king will need.

TARTUFFE Show the man no mercy!
Lock him up and lose the key!

MARIANE Well spoken, Monsieur Tartuffe.
It's most appropriate for you to be
The one to order me,
Because His majesty,
To stop this robbery,
Has just commissioned me

To issue this decree:
Arrest Tartuffe at once!

TARTUFFE What's that?!

ALL OTHERS All hail our noble king!
To thy majestic name we sing!

(TARTUFFE appeals in turn to the "BAILIFF," the "OFFICER" and to the "ENVOY," all of whom ignore him, joining the others in praising the king.)

TARTUFFE There's some mistake!
This cannot be!
That's the man you want!
Not me!

MARIANE Our prince knows all
The crimes that man commits,
And can't be fooled by wily hypocrites.
He long has known
The tricks Tartuffe employed;
This deed of gift he orders null and void!
(She tears up the deed.)

VALÈRE *(To TARTUFFE)* Come quickly, Sir,
Or I'll use force.

MARIANE Outside you'll find
A coach and horse.
The driver knows
The quickest course
To get you out of France
By break of day.
But if, by chance,
You disobey,
Or if, most miserable of men,
Your face is seen
In France again,
The sentence passed on you
Shall then prevail,
And you shall rot
Your life away in jail!

TARTUFFE *(As DAMIS and VALÈRE take hold of him)*
But what's the charge?
I'm not a crook.

(MARIANE produces a notebook from which she and then the others read.)

MARIANE Our sovereign knows your crimes;
They fill a dreadful book:

ORGON *(Reading)* Delinquent debts in Dijon,

ELMIRE Larcenous lies in Lyon,

DAMIS Treacherous acts in Toulouse,

DORINE Lecherous acts in Toulon.

(As the list is read, TARTUFFE backs off, and finally runs for his life.)

ALL *(Variously and together, except TARTUFFE)*
Embezzlement in Bordeaux,
Mortal sins in Marivaux;
Confidence games,
Anonymous names;
Thieving,
Deceiving,
Beyond all believing.
In Tours he was sought,
In Bourges he was caught;
A fraud in Ferrand,
A forger in Lot.
Fabrication,
Usurpation;
Provence,
Valence,
The Ile-de-France.
Stealing,
Concealing,
And bigamous dealing;
Beauvais,
Calais;
But now we've got him!
At last we've caught him!
Tyrant! Traitor!
Lecher! Liar! Lout!
Be gone forever!
Get out! Get out!

(TARTUFFE runs out. MARIANE, VALÈRE and DAMIS throw off their disguises and all break out in laughter. ORGON takes MARIANE on his arm and leads her, as in a wedding procession, across the stage to VALÈRE, to whom he gives her.)

ORGON Good people, I've been a fool.
Forgive me if you can.
Forgive me, Son.

DAMIS What's done is done.

ORGON Forgive me, Mariane.

ALL OTHERS All's well that ends well.

ORGON *(To VALÈRE)* Forgive me if you can.

ALL OTHERS Forget the past—
There's a wedding to plan!

ALL All's well that ends well;
The comedy ends as it should, with a song:
Love over hate,
Right over wrong;
The villain is gone,
The wedding is on.

MME. PERNELLE That man was so vile, I'm simply aghast!

ELMIRE & ORGON *(To Damis)* But how did you do it—
To catch him at last?

DAMIS The list that we drew
Of his crimes was all true;

DAM., VAL., MAR. Why else do you think that he ran off so fast?

ALL Fa la la, etc.

VALÈRE Fair Mariane I love and hourly I die,

MARIANE But not for a lip, nor a languishing eye.

VALÈRE She's faithful and true,

VALÈRE, MARIANE And there we agree,
For I'll be as true and as faithful as she (he).

ALL Fa la la, etc.
All's well that ends well;
The comedy ends as it should, with a song:
(Variously and together)
Long live the lovers!
Let's crown their delight
With dancing and singing
Far into the night.
Fa la la, etc.

MME. PERNELLE But now it is Heaven we ought to think of;
We must find a moral to this from above.

ORGON We've had enough morals and not enough love.

ALL OTHERS Now there is the moral we all need more of.

ALL Fa la la, etc.

End of the Opera